ANIMALS *in* DANGER

Black Rhino

Rod Theodorou

Heinemann Library
Chicago, Illinois

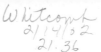

Designed by Ron Kamen
Illustrations by Dewi Morris/Robert Sydenham
Originated by Ambassador Litho
Printed by South China Printing in Hong Kong / China

05 04 03 02 01
10 9 8 7 6 5 4 3 2 1

Library of Congress Cataloging-in-Publication Data
Theodorou, Rod.
    Black rhino / Rod Theodorou.
       p.c m. – (Animals in danger)
       Includes bibliographical references (p.)
       ISBN 1-57572-262-3 (library)
       1. Black rhinoceros—Juvenile literature. 2. Endangered species—Juvenile literature. [1. Black rhinoceros. 2. Rhinoceros. 3. Endangered species.] I. Title.

QL737.U63 T44 2000
599.66'8—dc21
00-026775

Acknowledgments
The author and publishers are grateful to the following for permission to reproduce copyright material:Ardea London, p. 13, Ardea London/ R.F. Porter, p. 23; Corbis, p. 11; FLPA/ Gerard Lacz, p. 4, FLPA/ David Hosking, pp. 5, 22, FLPA/ W. Wisniewski, p. 6, FLPA/ Eichhorn Zingel, p. 8, FLPA/ Frants Hartmann, pp. 19, 21; Mike Johnson, p. 4; NHPA/ Martin Harvey, p. 18, NHPA/ Daryl Balfour, p. 25; Oxford Scientific Films, p. 16, Oxford Scientific Films/ Daniel J. Cox p. 4, Oxford Scientific Films/ Tom Leach pp. 7, 9, Oxford Scientific Films/ Stan Osolonski, p. 12, Oxford Scientific Films/ Konrad Wothe, p. 14, Oxford Scientific Films/ Steve Turner, pp. 15, 24, Oxford Scientific Films/ David Cayless, p. 20; Still Pictures/ M. & C. Denis-Huot, p.17, Still Pictures/ Michel Gunther, p. 26, Still Pictures/ Roland Seitre, p. 27

Cover photograph reproduced with permission of Bruce Coleman.
Special thanks to Henning Dräger for his comments in the preparation of this book.

Every effort has been made to contact copyright holders of any material reproduced in this book. Any omissions will be rectified in subsequent printings if notice is given to the publisher.

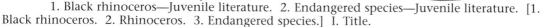

Some words are shown in bold, **like this.** You can find out what they mean by looking in the glossary.

Contents

Animals in Danger

blue whale

Bengal tiger

manatee

All over the world, more than 10,000 animal **species** are in danger. Some are in danger because their homes are being destroyed. Many are in danger because people hunt them.

4

This book is about black rhinos and why they are **endangered**. Unless people learn to **protect** them, black rhinos will become **extinct**. We will only be able to find out about them from books like this.

What Is a Rhino?

Rhinos are huge **mammals**. There are five different **species** of rhino. The two largest species are the black rhino and the white rhino. This picture shows a white rhino.

They are called black and white rhinos, but both species are gray. White rhinos have wide, square lips. Black rhinos have a pointed, hooked lip like a parrot's beak. This picture shows a black rhino.

What Does a Rhino Look Like?

Rhinos have huge bodies. They have four short thick legs with three stumpy toes on each leg. Their skin is gray and very thick, like armor. They are heavy, but they can move very quickly.

Some rhinos have only one horn, but the black rhino has two horns. The horns are very hard and are used to protect the rhino from **predators.** A black rhino's horn can grow longer than a baseball bat!

W:..r: no A:.inos Liv:?

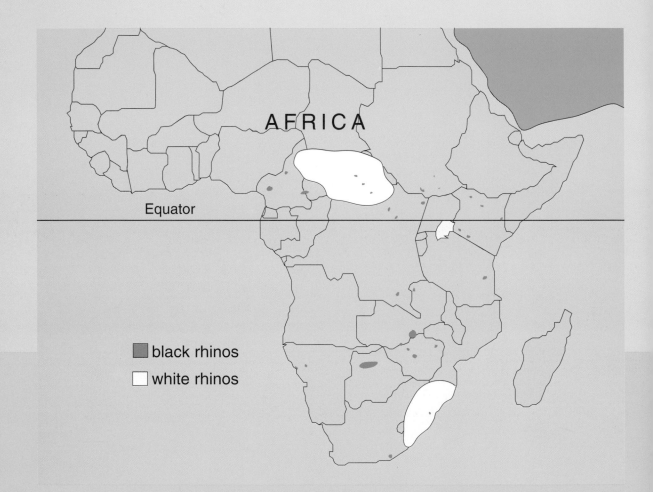

AFRICA

Equator

black rhinos
white rhinos

Black and white rhinos both live in Africa. White rhinos like open **savannah** where they can eat lots of grass. Black rhinos like to live on the edge of forests near bushes and trees.

The Indian, Javan, and Sumatran rhinos live in Asia. The Javan and Sumatran rhinos live deep inside rain forests where they can find leaves and fruit to eat. The Indian rhino likes wallowing in cool, muddy swamps and marshes.

What Do Black Rhinos Eat?

Rhinos are **herbivores**. They only eat plants and fruits. Black rhinos use their hooked lips to pluck off leaves or pull down small trees to eat the fruit.

Black rhinos eat in the morning and late into the evening. They do not like the hot sun. They find a shady place to rest in during the heat of the day.

Black Rhino Babies

Black rhinos do not live in family groups. They like to live alone and are only together to **mate**. When they have mated the **male** leaves. He does not help take care of the baby.

The **female** usually only has one baby. The baby is called a calf. The calf can stand up about an hour after it is born. It feeds on its mother's milk.

Caring for the Calf

The calf's horn is only a small bump at first, but it grows quickly. The calf will live with its mother for two or three years, and then it will live on its own.

Hyenas and lions sometimes attack black rhino calves. The mother will charge at any **predator** that comes near her calf. Black rhinos are very fierce when they feel they are in danger.

Unusual Rhino Facts

Black rhinos cannot see very well, but they have a very good sense of smell. They only have hair on the ends of their tails, on their eyelashes, and on the tips of their ears.

White rhinos live in **herds** and are not very dangerous. Black rhinos live alone and sometimes may charge people who come too close.

How Many Black Rhinos Are There?

One hundred years ago there were about one million black rhinos in Africa. Now there are fewer than 1,900 of them in the wild, even though they are **protected** by **law**.

Black rhinos are being killed faster than any other large animal on Earth. Over 73,000 have been killed in the last 30 years!

Why Is the Black Rhino in Danger?

People shoot black rhinos and then cut off their horns to sell them. Many horns go to China to be **ground** down and sold as medicine.

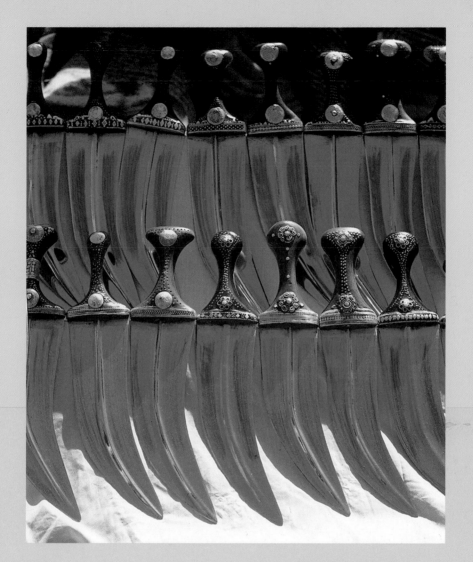

Many horns are sold to a country called Yemen. They are made into the handles of **daggers,** like the ones in this picture.

How Is the Black Rhino Being Helped?

Many leaders in China and Yemen are trying to stop sales of rhino horn. All African and Asian countries have made rhino hunting against the **law.** This black rhino has his own guard!

24

Conservation groups like the World Wildlife Fund (WWF) and the International Rhino Foundation (IRF) are also working to stop **poaching** and save the rhino.

In some countries black rhinos are caught and their horns are cut off and burned. This does not hurt the rhino, and it stops hunters from **poaching** them until the horns grow back.

Many African countries have places where the rhinos are **protected** by fences and guards. This is the best way to save the black rhino.

Rhino Fact File

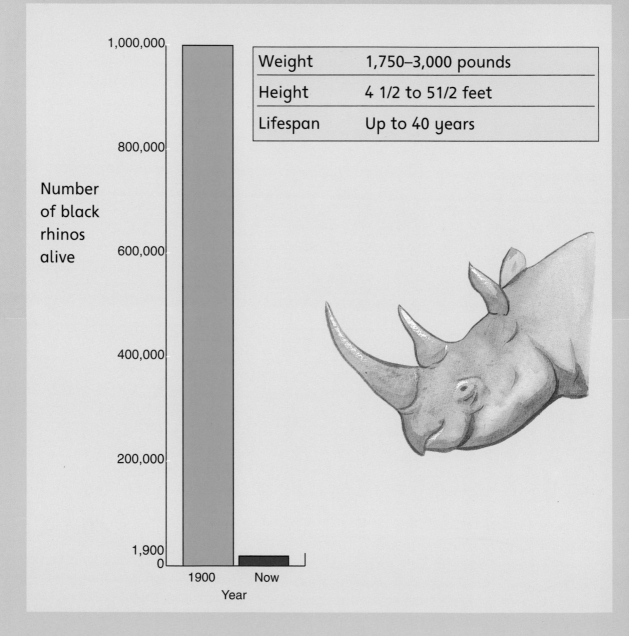

Weight	1,750–3,000 pounds	
Height	4 1/2 to 51/2 feet	
Lifespan	Up to 40 years	

Number of black rhinos alive

1,000,000
800,000
600,000
400,000
200,000
1,900
0

1900   Now
Year

World Danger Table

	Number that may have been alive 100 years ago	Number that may be alive today
Giant panda	65,000	650
Bengal tiger	100,000	4,500
Blue whale	335,000	4,000
Mountain gorilla	85,000	500
Florida manatee	75,000	2,000

There are thousands of other animals in the world that are in danger of becoming **extinct**. This table shows some of these animals.

How Can You Help the Black Rhino?

If you and your friends raise money for the rhinos, you can send it to these groups. They will take the money and use it to pay guards, and to buy food and tools to help save the black rhino.

Defenders of Wildlife
1101 Fourteenth Street, N.W. #1400
Washington, DC 20005

International Rhino Foundation
14000 International Rd.
Cumberland, OH 43732

World Wildlife Fund
1250 Twenty-fourth Street, N.W.
P.O. Box 97180
Washington, DC 20037

More Books to Read

Fichter, George S. *Endangered Animals.* New York, N.Y.: Golden Books
   Publishing Company, 1995.

National Wildlife Federation Staff. *Endangered Species: Wild & Rare.*
   Broomall, Penn.: Chelsea House Publishers, 1999. An older reader can
   help you with this book.

Glossary

dagger	sharp, pointed knife with a handle
endangered	group of animals that is dying out, so there are few left
extinct	group of animals that has completely died out and can never live again
female	girl or woman
ground	crushed into powder
herbivore	animal that eats only plants
herd	group of the same animals living together
law	rule or something you have to do
mammal	warm-blooded animals, like humans, that feed their young on their mother's milk
male	boy or man
mate	when a male animal and a female animal come together to make baby animals
poacher/poaching	hunter who makes money from hunting (poaching) animals to sell parts of their bodies like teeth, bones, and fur
predator	animal that hunts and kills other animals
protected	kept safe
savannah	large area of grassland with few trees
species	group of living things that are very similar

Index